SEVEN COUNTRY DANCES
FOR FLUTE & PIANO
RICHARD RODNEY BENNETT

NOVELLO

CONTENTS

Cover design: Fresh Lemon
Music setting: Robin Hagues
Photograph of Richard Rodney Bennett by Katie van Dyck

NOV121297
ISBN 1-84609-166-7

Head office
14/15 Berners Street, London W1T 3LJ, England
Tel: +44 (0)20 7612 7400
Fax: +44 (0)20 7612 7545

Sales and hire
Music Sales Limited,
Newmarket Road, Bury St Edmunds, Suffolk IP33 3YB, England
Tel: +44 (0)1284 702600
Fax: +44 (0)1284 768301

www.chesternovello.com
e-mail: music@musicsales.co.uk

SEVEN COUNTRY DANCES

Richard Rodney Bennett
arr. Elizabeth Robinson

1. All in a garden green

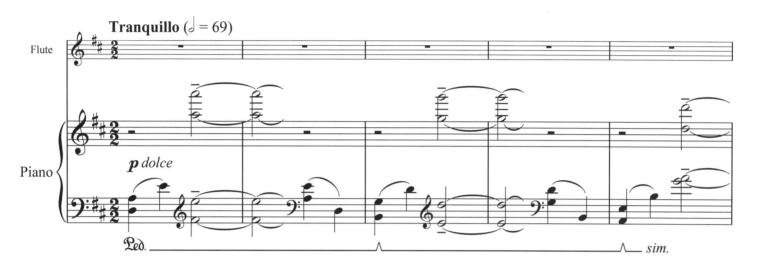

4

2. The Ladies' Misfortune

3. Buskin

* 'Old Noll's Jig'

4. Lady Day

SEVEN COUNTRY DANCES

FOR FLUTE & PIANO
RICHARD RODNEY BENNETT

NOVELLO

CONTENTS

Cover design: Fresh Lemon
Music setting: Robin Hagues
Photograph of Richard Rodney Bennett by Katie van Dyck

NOV121297
ISBN 1-84609-166-7

Head office
14/15 Berners Street, London W1T 3LJ, England
Tel: +44 (0)20 7612 7400
Fax: +44 (0)20 7612 7545

Sales and hire
Music Sales Limited,
Newmarket Road, Bury St Edmunds, Suffolk IP33 3YB, England
Tel: +44 (0)1284 702600
Fax: +44 (0)1284 768301

www.chesternovello.com
e-mail: music@musicsales.co.uk

SEVEN COUNTRY DANCES

Richard Rodney Bennett
arr. Elizabeth Robinson

1. All in a garden green

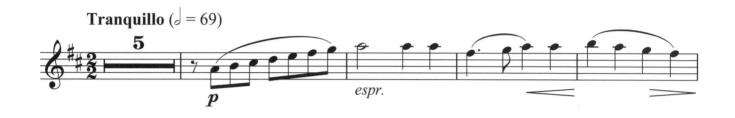

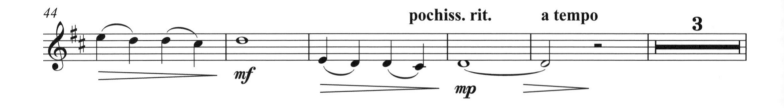

2. The Ladies' Misfortune

3. Buskin

Vivo e ritmico ($\quarternote$ = 120)

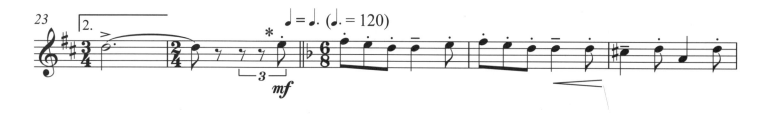

* 'Old Noll's Jig'

4. Lady Day

* can be played on flutes with a low B foot joint

5. The Mulberry Garden

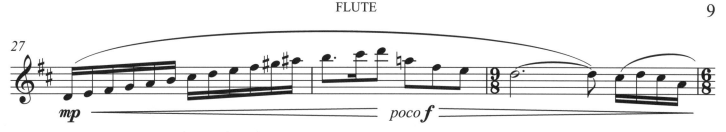

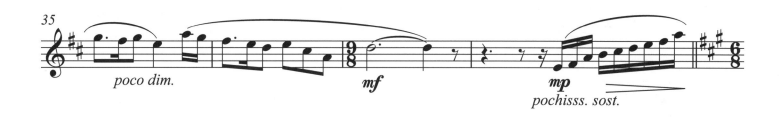

6. Nobody's Jig

7. Chelsea Reach

123456789

FLUTE MUSIC FROM CHESTER/NOVELLO

Flute and Piano

Rupert Bawden
Railings
NOV120823

Richard Rodney Bennett
Suite Française
NOV952886

Summer Music
NOV120560

Lennox Berkeley
Concerto for Flute
and Orchestra, Op. 36
CH01591

Sonata for Flute
CH55183

A Couperin Flute Album
ed. Trevor Wye
NOV120609

Franz Doppler
Hungarian Pastoral Fantasy, Op.26
ed. Trevor Wye
CH55164

An Elgar Flute Album
ed. Trevor Wye
NOV120553

Gabriel Faure
Fantasie, Op. 79
CH55163

Flute Encores
An album of pieces by Terschak,
Reichert, Briccialdi, Boehm, J.S. Bach
and Köhler, ed. Trevor Wye
CH55194

James Galway Showpieces
An album of pieces by Bach,
Chopin, Doppler, Drigo, Gluck,
Godard, Michio Miyagi,
Paganini, Rimsky-Korsakoff
and Saint-Saëns.
NOV120472

Benjamin Godard
Suite de Trois Morceaux Op.116
ed. Trevor Wye
CH55136

Eugene Goossens
Three Pictures
CT01559

Dave Heath
Out of the Cool
CH55693

Bryan Kelly
Sonatina
CH55286

Tristan Keuris
Aria
NOV120652

John McCabe
Portraits
NOV120529

Elizabeth Maconchy
Colloquy
CH55229

The Magic Flute of James Galway
An album of pieces by Bach, Briccialdi,
Chopin, Dvorak, Gossec, Handel, Kreisler,
Mendelssohn, Rachmaninoff and Schumann,
arranged for flute and piano.
NOV120498

Mozart
Concerto No. 1 in G, K.313
ed. Trevor Wye
NOV120577

Francis Poulenc
Sonata for Flute and Piano
CH01605

A Satie Flute Album
ed. Trevor Wye
NOV120554

Robert Saxton
Krystallen
CH55691

A Schumann Flute Album
NOV120562

Gerard Schurmann
Sonatina
NOV120395

A Vivaldi Album
ed. Trevor Wye
NOV120603

Solo Flute

Theobald Boehm
Twenty-four Capriccios
for solo flute
ed. Trevor Wye
CH55209

The Orchestral Flute Practice
Book 1 (A-P)
NOV120801
Book 2 (R-Z)
ed. Trevor Wye & Patricia Morris
NOV120802

Francis Poulenc
Un Joueur de flûte
berce les ruines
CH61753

Claude Debussy
Syrinx
ed. Trevor Wye
NOV120756

5. The Mulberry Garden

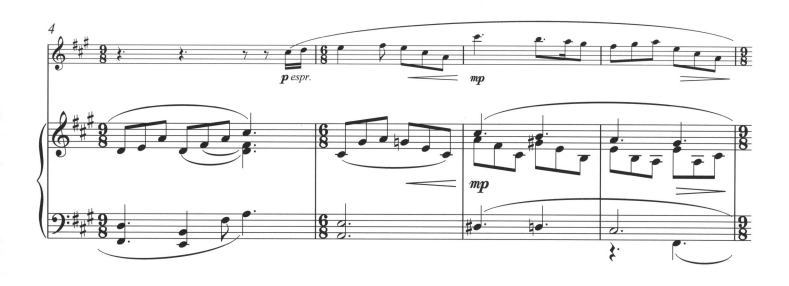

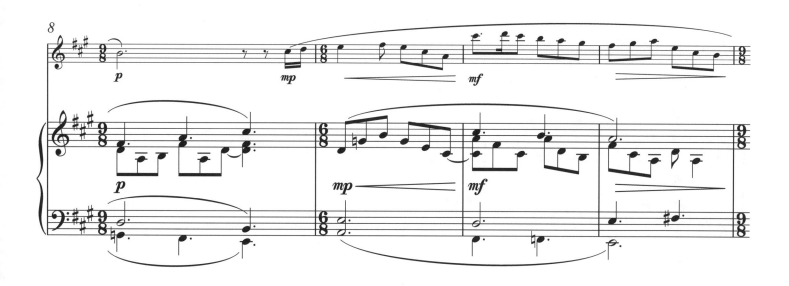

6. Nobody's Jig

24

7. Chelsea Reach